THE SECRET LIFE OF CATS

ROBERT   DE   LAROCHE   •   JEAN-MICHEL   LABAT

MYTHIC ORIGINS

In creation myths, the cat is universally linked to the mother goddesses and to the stars of Day and Night.

Those with imaginations claim that the cat came from Atlantis. Cats are not mentioned in the Bible. The Muslims believe the cat first appeared on Noah's Ark when, pestered by numerous rats infesting the boat, the old man asked God's advice. He was ordered to hit the lion's muzzle, causing the beast to sneeze forth the first pair of cats.

Mohammed is supposed to have bestowed upon the cat one of its remarkable abilities. One day, when the prophet was preparing himself for prayer he found that his cat, Muezza, was sleeping on his robe; unwilling to disturb the creature, the prophet tore off the sleeve on which she rested. On his return, Muezza expressed her gratitude with a deep bow. In order to acknowledge this display of exquisite politeness, Mohammed granted to the cat and others like it the gift of always landing on their feet.

In Buddhism, which traces its origins back to antiquity, the cat occupies an equivocal position, attributed to an incident that took place at the time of the Buddha's death. All the animals gathered, weeping, around the sacred reamains; only the snake and the cat remained dry eyed.

The mythology of Greece and Rome followed that of Egypt in attributing the cat's origins to the divinities of the moon, Artemis and Diana.

Under the influence of Christianity, Western mythology replaced the duality of sun and moon with the Manichaean conflict of good versus evil. Thus the dog is a creation of God and the cat the work of the devil. Another version holds that the cat is privileged with knowing the path back to the Garden of Eden. Amid the general misery that accompanied the expulsion of Adam and Eve and their children from Paradise, the cat was the only one to make a note of the route. Touched by the tears of Jacob, the third son of the First Parents, he led the little boy to the gates of Heaven. From that time on, it is said, there is always somewhere in the world a child and a cat who know the secret of the way back to the Garden of Eden.

IN THE CAT'S FOOTSTEPS

Ten thousand years before Christ, man exchanged his nomadic existence for a settled one, began to cultivate the earth and to tame various animals. Cultivation brought with it rodents, and these in turn attracted predators.

The earliest known cat remains associated with human settlement were found on the site of Jericho in Palestine and date from 6700 B.C. Later traces, dating back to 2000 B.C., were found during the excavations of Harappa in the Indus Valley. Cat remains dating from nearly 5000 B.C. have also been found in Cyprus; these were almost certainly animals imported from the Orient.

There is a theory that the cat came to Egypt, already domesticated, from Pakistan or Persia. One tradition suggests that cats had been domesticated in Egypt as early as the Third and Fourth Dynasties, *c.* 2600 B.C., the time of the pyramid-building pharaohs Zoser, Cheops, Chephren, and Mycerinus. Their titanic monuments are thought to have been built by a huge workforce of Nubian slaves. The gloved cats that frequented their settlements in what is now the Sudan may have followed them to the sites of Saqqarah and Giza. At first subsisting on the fish of the Nile and the birds that nested among the papyrus reeds, the cats would soon have attached themselves to the local peasants, protecting their granaries and ridding their homes of the various rodents that infested them.

From the time of the New Empire and the Eighteenth Dynasty (*c.* 1500 B.C.), the cat assumed an important role in the religious and daily life of Egypt. The earliest known cat sarcophagus dates from the Eighteenth Dynasty and comes from Saqqarah. Sculpted in limestone, it shows several feline effigies surrounding the goddesses Isis and Nephthys. The inscriptions reveal that the sarcophagus contained the body of a female cat belonging to one of the high priests of Memphis. The custom of mummifying and interring cats reached its height when the cult of Bastet came to the fore under the pharaohs of Bubastis (*c.* 950 B.C.). Most of the surviving mummies date from a later period. As late as 500 B.C. the cat was almost unknown in Greece, where weasels, ferrets, and grass snakes watched over the crops. Then the Greeks began to mount covert expeditions to steal cats from Egypt. A flourishing trade later developed, with Phoenician and Greek merchants selling Oriental cats to private individuals, often at exorbitant prices.

Valued for its usefulness and its beauty, the cat pursued its route into

Cats were mummified in great quantities in Egypt, some being killed for that purpose.

6

Europe by way of Italy. The cat became integrated into Roman society as a familiar companion, a children's pet and *genius loci*. Its independent nature appealed to the Romans so much that in the second century B.C. a cat was shown at the foot of a statue of the Goddess of Liberty in a temple in Rome.

For a long time some writers maintained that cats were unknown to the Gauls and barely known to the Celts, in whose lands they had appeared only briefly at the time of the Roman conquest, and that they did not become established in northern Europe until the turn of the tenth century. But this theory overlooks various Gallo-Roman sculptures in which cats appear. Cat remains have been discovered in the burial pits of a Gallo-Roman villa in southwest France, while a Merovingian village in the north has yielded evidence of cats and dogs living alongside men.

Cats seem to have been common in Saxon England, where numerous skeletons dating from the early seventh century indicate that the cat was already well established as a domestic animal. In about 945 A.D. the Welsh king Hywel Dda (or Howell the Good) passed a series of laws aimed at protecting the cat, mainly to prevent their theft and torture but also probably to halt the widespread practice of killing them for their coats, which were highly prized by furriers. However, it was not until the fourteenth century, that a distinction was made between the trade in "skins of wild cats" and those of "the private cats called hearth or household cats."

THE NAME OF THE CAT

In addition to the many other mysteries and conjectures surrounding the cat, its very name is an enigma. The origin of the word "cat" continues to provoke almost as much disagreement among linguists.

The ancient Egyptians referred to the cat by *myeou* or *miou,* a phonetic transcription of the animal's hieroglyph that depicted it seated in profile. Certain funerary inscriptions give the term *techau,* indicating a female cat.

It has also been suggested the French *matou* — tomcat — is an anagram of Atum (spelled Atoum in French), an Egyptian sun deity linked to the cat.

Other lexicographers trace the origin of the word "pussy" to the Egyptian Pasht, one of the names for Bastet.

In Latin, *felis* meant cat, Cicero being the first to use it in this precise sense in the first century A.D. *Felis* is of course the origin of our word "feline," but "cat" and the French *chat* come from *cattus,* later *catus,* a word of uncertain origin, first used in the low Latin of Palladius in the fourth century A.D.

Whatever its origin, it was *cattus* that prevailed, reappearing in numerous guises: *gato* (Portuguese and Spanish), *gatto* (Italian), *chat* (French), *kochka* (Russian), *Katze* or *Kater* (German), and, of course, our own word "cat."

The cat has enriched our language in a whole array of proverbs and metaphors. Many are no longer in common use, as for example "to turn the cat in the pan," which means "to make black white" or, "to change sides." Others testify to some well-known characteristic of the animal: its calculating prudence ("wait to see which way the cat jumps"), its alleged inscrutability ("to make a cat laugh"), its vigilance ("when the cat's away, the mice will play"), or its penchant for having some sport with its prey before killing it ("playing cat and mouse"). As everyone knows, "a cat in gloves catches no mice," i.e., restraint and caution ("pussyfooting") achieves nothing, while "there is more than one way to skin a cat."

COMPANION ON THE FINAL VOYAGE

Always alert, even when fast asleep, the watchful cat was believed by the Egyptians to be one of the privileged guardians of the doors of the night and the kingdom beyond. The sacred texts' description of the Great Cat or Great Tomcat makes him sound like a humorous creature. The divine cat has a heroic role in a crucial episode of the night voyage of the divine boat, a drama played out each night after Ra, the sun, sinks into sleep and passes the gates of the underworld, accompanied by a cortège of the righteous dead. In Amenta, the kingdom of the dead, Ra, now helpless, passes the night hours. At the eighth hour Apep, an emanation of Seth, a slippery and malevolent serpent, tries to stop the divine boat. The invincible guardian, the Great Cat, appears, cuts off the head of Apep, and the divine boat continues on its course. This struggle of light and shade was reenacted each night, an eternal conflict that mirrored the equilibrium of the universe.

This power of the cat over the forces of darkness is shown in statuary. Egyptian priests thought to confer on certain statues a life of their own by depicting them with open eyes and mouths. The stone, touched by the breath of life, thus possessed "a heart and a *ka* (life force)," and the living statue — the word is a translation of the Egyptian *shespankh,* meaning sphinx — drew into itself a measure of divine power.

Like the lion, the cat had the power to purge the atmosphere of evil

exhalations, both in temples and in homes, where it kept particular vigil over sleepers in the same way as the Great Cat protected Ra. The fact that the Egyptians should have chosen as Guardian of Sleep an animal that spends around 70 percent of its existence asleep and dreams for up to four hours each day is an indication that the study of cat behavior was really far advanced in the Pharaonic period!

There were several other cat necropolises at Saqqarah, Beni-Hassan, Stabl Antar, and it was supposed until recently that cats that died, whether in temples or in private households, were embalmed, mummified — some being placed in sarcophagi — and then buried in one of the cemeteries consecrated to the animal.

Researchers have also discovered elongation and fracture marks in the cervical vertebrae of some mummified cats, proving that the animals had been deliberately killed. Was this a case of ritual sacrifice or, more prosaically, was it a question of ensuring an adequate supply of raw material for the pilgrims' mummies? In the absence of documentation, the uncertainty persists.

Egyptian cat in bronze.

This role as guardian of the threshold has been assigned to the cat across the ages, and in diverse civilizations. One cannot remain unmoved by the presence of such large numbers of cats in cemeteries all over the world.

In Greece, where its role was that of a children's pet, the cat seems to have been linked with its protégé even after death, as is shown in the funerary stele of Salamine (420 B.C.), which depicts a young child and a cat. This Greek image is an isolated case, but later examples have come to light throughout the Roman world. Several steles found in France depict similar themes.

But the most touching image from the Gallo-Roman era is surely the so-called stele of Laetus, found in the Roman wall of Bordeaux in 1831. A little girl holds a kitten that is drawing itself away from a cock that pecks the tip of its tail. This vivid scene seems to support the theory that it was customary for the Romans and Gauls, who buried their children along with their toys, also to represent them on memorials accompanied by their pets.

Funerary stele of Laetus.
Limestone, late first or early
second century A.D.

BASTET, THE DIVINE MOTHER

I am born of the divine She-cat, conceived beneath the sycamore of the enclosure by the seed come from on high, that my divinity may never be denied... I am born of the sacred She-cat, but I am also become a son of the Sun... born of the She-cat, I am the chief, the son of the She-cat, the double-guide, who will for his mother eternally remain the little one saved by the She-cat.

Thus does Osiris express himself in the Book of the Dead, indicating the feline nature of his divine mother, Nut, goddess of heaven.

Since earliest times, the cat, Pupil of Ra and Eye of Horus, fruitful warmth of the sun and fertility linked to the moon, has been associated with maternity. The Egyptians were certainly struck by cats' reproductive capacity, the legendary nature of which Plutarch would subsequently emphasize:

It is said in fact that this animal makes one baby, then two, then three, then four, then five, and thus as many as seven at a time, such that in all it can go as far as twentyeight, *a number equal to that of the days of the moon.*

As Egyptian theology evolved and was modified, the sacred She-cat would be particularly identified with Isis, Hathor, and Sekhmet the lioness, whose benign aspect was represented by Bastet, the cat-goddess who sprang from the Eye of the Sun.

When Pharaoh Sheshank I, founder of the Twentysecond Dynasty c. 950 B.C., chose as his capital the city called Bubastis in Greek (Tell Basta in modern Egyptian), Bastet became the greatest divinity of the kingdom. Like all the temples of Pharaonic Egypt, Per Bast was open to the faithful only during religious festivals; on other days the priests and priestesses of Bastet celebrated the cult of the divine mother in deepest secret. In the second month of the season of Inundation, the Temple was a place of pilgrimage attracting hundreds of thousands of visitors each year for the Feast of Bastet. These celebrations, to which the people of the countryside journeyed by boat, took place in a climate of jubilation and freedom. The passengers, dancing to the sound of singing and castanets, insulted the people they saw on the banks, while the women provoked them by hitching up their skirts and shouting out obscenities — this feigned aggression was, no doubt, a means of reenacting the myth of Sekhmet the Violent, transported down the Nile on a boat to become the gentle Bastet of the south, and dispensing fertility on her way.

What, then, was Bastet's status? Goddess of music, of dance and of *joie-de-vivre,* she was at first the protectress

and nurse of the royal children, then goddess of maternity, and finally protectress of the entire Egyptian people. She was to become a goddess of immense prestige, as is borne out by the various epithets accorded her on temple steles, parchments, and sculptures. Bastet was "Lady of Heaven," "Lady of the Casket, initiated into the mysteries of Atum," "the White One, nurse of the Great Castle," "Great Conjuress of the Casket," "Mistress of the Oudjat Eye."

She protected pregnant women, watched over the gestation period, aided labor, suckled babies, and acted as nurse. Babies and infants were not the only ones to benefit from the goddess' indulgence; her protection continued as far as the adolescence of the young ones she had, symbolically, brought into the world.

Cat silhouettes were tattooed on children's arms, to evoke the goddess' redemptive presence, and the temple magicians even injected infants with a few drops of blood from sacred cats, to protect them from epidemics or harmful influences. During the Libyan and Kush eras, numerous children were given names that incorporated that of Bastet, such as Nes-Bastet ("the one of Bastet") or even Djed-Bastet-iouef-ankh ("Bastet said 'let him live' ").

A HOUSEHOLD SPIRIT

Just as the cat was a guardian of the threshold for the Egyptians, so it seems to have been considered as a *genius loci*, or household spirit, by the Gallo-Romans. A discovery made in 1937 at Alise-Sainte-Reine (Roman Alesia) supports this view. In the cellar of a private dwelling, in a room used for the practice of domestic cults, was found the leg of an offertory table dating from the second or third century A.D. The sculpture represents a smiling young man with abundant hair, wearing a toga that is raised to reveal the lower half of his body, up to his genitals. Folded in his garment he is cradling an out-stretched cat, which is wearing a bell collar around its neck.

Several examples of this kind of sculpted pedestal, which probably supported tables on which offerings of fruit were deposited, were found on the site of Alesia, in basement rooms generally given over to the worship of the Mater, protective goddess of the family. For the Romans, these *genii* (from *generare,* to engender) represented the life principle that ensured the perpetuity of the dynasty.

As for the cat, we know that the Gauls represented animals on their statues to emphasize certain qualities: strength, agility, and so on. In this case the cat was probably chosen as a symbol of fertility, and also, perhaps, for its power to ward off evil spirits, as seems to be suggested by the bell around its neck.

Young man with cat found in 1937 on the site of Roman Alesia (second or third century A.D.).

NINE LIVES OR NINE TAILS?

Everyone knows that a cat has nine lives. At least, this is a country belief that still persists and contributes to the aura of mystery surrounding the cat. The idea that the cat can reincarnate itself makes sense to those who believe it to be a magical animal.

It's also possible that the cat's hardy resistance to pain and illness gave rise to its reputation for having several lives. The English seem to have perpetuated this belief in the nineteenth century, in the nickname for the whip: "cat-o'-nine-tails."

But the key to this belief is to be found much further back in history, in ancient Egypt. In many cosmogonies the number nine is of paramount importance. It is the number that represents the sum total, universality, achievement. Pharaonic religion was no exception to this "rule of nine."

Atum-Ra, the creating sun, gave birth to two couples: Shu (air) and Tefnut (moisture); and Geb (earth) and Nut (sky), his wife. These last, in turn, begat Osiris and Isis, Seth and Nephthys. As the author of a religious text from Deir el-Bahari, dating from the Twentysecond Dynasty, proclaims: "I am one who becomes two; I am two who become four; I am four who become eight; I am one more after that." The primordial nine thus represents a unity.

A hymn from the fourth century B.C. addressed to Ra, the sun of Heliopolis, offers a key to this puzzle. It runs: "O sacred cat! Your mouth is the mouth of the god Atum, the lord of life who has saved you from all taint." Thus the cat is invested with the creative power of Atum-Ra, the unique, who is nine even as he is one. Doubtless it was for this reason that the Egyptian priests, and thenceforth popular superstition, began to credit the cat with the privilege of nine successive lives.

CRICKET ON THE HEARTH

The cat, household god and protective spirit of the family, soon gravitated to the very heart of the house, the hearth. Traditionally this was the entrance and exit for both good and bad spirits, for the sorceress as well as for Santa Claus. The cat has tamed fire, and it is proud of its conquest. And the peasants whose homes it shared were quick to notice this fondness for the hearth, the focus of household life. A cat new to the house was immediately taken to the hearth to ensure that it would not run away. This introduction to the heart of the house was completed by an offering of food.

The cat, however, had to defend its place at the fireside against its eternal enemy. The story of the war between cats and dogs for possession of the hearth is passed down in a Walloon legend. Dogs and cats went to settle their differences before the tribunal of St. Peter and the verdict was recorded on a piece of parchment: The cat was granted the 12 night hours by the hearth, while dogs

could claim possession during the day. With characteristic cunning the cats progressively encroached on the daytime period, and one can be fairly sure that the conflict will continue until the end of time.

BEWARE THE BLACK CAT

Throughout history, no animal close to man has so vividly evoked his fear of the unknown, his terror of the dark, his complicity with the devil, as — inadvertently — the black cat.

Having achieved divine status in Ancient Egypt, the cat arrived in Europe shrouded in mystery. Associated with the last priestesses of lunar cults, it was viewed as an alien of unknown origin whose intense and indefinable presence disturbed the newly established order of Christianity. Pagan cults had been banned since the fourth century; in 557 A.D. the Council of Tours forbade Christians, under pain of excommunication, to make sacrifices to the dead or to indulge in any of the other rituals disapproved of by the Church.

The first victims of these edicts were the wise women and folk-healers, experts in the art of curing with natural remedies, who had inherited the healing functions of the earth-mother goddesses along with their symbol. Their familiar was, naturally, a black cat.

The general panic that preceded the coming of the millennium and its anticipated catastrophes exposed the cat to the full animosity of the clergy. Two centuries later, the return of the Crusaders and the epidemics of black plague heralded the doleful period of cat massacres. The only ones to escape the holocaust were those cats who had a tuft of white hair in their black coat, usually situated on the breast. This mark of innocence was called the "angel's mark" or "God's finger," and inspired the torturers to mercy; hence the relative rarity today of absolutely black cats, these massacres having operated as a form of selection.

OLD WIVES TALES

A black cat crossing your path brings misfortune, especially if it comes from the left. There are an alarming number of superstitions engendered by the cat, most of which are thankfully forgotten. Each country region has its own. Although the cat was tolerated on farms for its rat-catching abilities, it remained a mysterious animal inspiring little or no trust, thus the saying: "The dog wakes thrice to watch over his master, the cat wakes thrice to strangle him."

In the Vosges, to meet a cat on the first day of the year was to be doomed to 365 days of bad luck; in Normandy, superstitious businessmen, on their way to settle a deal, would abandon the expedition if they happened to see a cat on the way. In Provence, the innocent spectacle of cats playing in the morning was the harbinger of a wasted day. Walloons mistrusted any cat who came to be petted; it was the sure sign of a

coming betrayal. In Brittany, people avoided confiding secrets in the presence of a cat, even if it was asleep, for fear that the secret would soon be spread abroad.

In Anjou, this animal of ill omen was supposedly capable of preventing bread from rising (or of causing it to burn).

In spite of all this, a cat's death was everywhere considered to presage misfortune. In Germany, two cats fighting in front of a sick person's dwelling meant that the invalid would shortly die, and the presence of a black cat on a gravestone indicated that the devil had taken possession of the soul of the departed. In Tuscany, people avoided reference to a deceased person for fear of seeing him appear with a cat's face. In contrast, in Sicily, no one would ever have thought of mistreating a cat, for the animal was considered sacred to St. Martha.

If you can work up the courage, go at midnight to a forest on the night of the full moon and there, where four paths meet, call up the devil. He will appear to you in the form of a black cat. A few drops of blood from your left hand at the bottom of a parchment, and buried treasure and riches unimaginable are yours. You have nothing to lose — except, of course, in the end, your immortal soul…

This was common belief in the countryside not so long ago, and it was thought that the cat was the guardian of buried treasure.

Cats were thought to be privy to the arcane secrets of the gold of knowledge, a sort of "cat who laid the golden egg."

How can you tell a gold-bringing cat from an ordinary cat? It must be: black, naturally, and lazy, not inclined to chase mice. It played its real role only after nightfall. In some regions it was thought that the magic would work only if the mistress of the house offered the cat her breast and suckled it. But generally it was enough to place a purse containing a golden coin next to the cat before going to bed, and whisper in its ear: "Do your duty." Come morning the purse would be filled with gold pieces.

AT THE SIGN OF THE CAT

The cat had happier associations in European folklore than those suggested by its ritual burning. It was, for instance, a common feature of the signs that hung above the entrances to numerous workshops in the little streets of medieval towns.

Punning images were a feature of heraldry, and the cat has played its part in the symbolism. In the fifth century the cat was adopted as a symbol of liberty and independence by Gundiracus, King of Burgundy. And in due course the cat came to feature on more than a hundred European coats-of-arms (often with a punning meaning, like Balzac's cat — in heraldry this is called canting) such as those of the families of Lechat, Gatti, Katzen, Lecat, and Katzmair.

The cat has never enjoyed the same popularity in heraldic representation as its larger relative, the lion. Nevertheless,

whether crouching in fear or rampant (upright on its back legs), bristling (back raised, fur erect), or armed (with claws of a different color from the body), a cat in a coat-of-arms represents at least as much as the lion those qualities of independence and freedom for which it is famed.

THE CELESTIAL CAT

To the Egyptians the cat was a divine creature, born in the heart of Heaven, the site of the constellation of the Lion. This divinity arrived in the Nubian desert in the shape of a blood-thirsty lioness. Variously identified with Hathor, Tefnut, and above all with Sekhmet ("the Powerful One"), wife of Ptah, this divine harridan revelled in a frenzy of slaughter. Then Ra sent the warrior god Enouris to earth with orders to curb Sekhmet. Once tamed, the lioness transformed herself into a cat, the goddess Bastet.

Western astronomy neglected *Felis catus*. At the end of the eighteenth century, the French astronomer Joseph-Jérôme Lalande, in rearranging the stars into different constellations, nominated the cat for a small one.

In Chinese astrology, as popularized in the West, the cat does indeed have a place among the animals of the Zodiac, if only as a substitute, because this fourth sign, corresponding to our Cancer, is more properly called the hare.

The cat makes a spectacular appearance on the last image of the tarot's major card, the Fool. This card shows a vagabond. His shoes are torn, and a white and red cat is biting his leg. According to one tradition, tarot originated in Egypt. Other authorities hold that it originated in Venice, the source of the earliest known game, dating from the fourteenth century. Cats were venerated in both places, and there is nothing surprising about the presence on the card of a cat warning mankind against the good and evil powers of the nocturnal world.

Some have seen the Fool as a representation of unconscious man, blind to the knowledge tied up in his beggar's bag. But he can also be a wise man, an initiate, a master, one who feels the need to retire from the solar world, to meditate in lonely places bathed in the clear light of the moon toward which he is advancing.

THE ALCHEMICAL CAT

The cat was admitted into the secret of the alchemist's cabinet, as is evident from the engraving on the flyleaf of Lambsprinck's treatise, *De Lapide Philosophico* (The Philosopher's Stone, 1677). This depicts a majestic white cat emerging from a cave, inside which a dragon lurks, and above which we see the sun god Jupiter.

Mythology has made the cat a repository of secrets, because the X shape of its whiskers represents the Greek letter *khi*, the initial letter of *chaos* (the alchemist's *prima materia*), and also of the Greek words for crucible, gold, and time — the triple unknown of the Grand Design. Thus the X formed by the cat's whiskers represents "light formed by light." The variations in the color of the cat's coat can also be interpreted as symbolic of different phases of the Design. When it is black, it suggests raw material; when russet, it symbolizes secret fire.

Thirteenth-century stallcarving.
Poitiers Cathedral, France.

THE ECCLESIASTICAL CAT

Although the Church, in the person of Pope Gregory IX and subsequent accusers, set itself firmly against the cat throughout the Middle Ages, it would be wrong to assume that every priest, monk, and nun reacted in the same way. There is a considerable body of evidence, from illustrated manuscripts, miniatures, and church carvings, testifying to the presence of cats.

This secret alliance appears to have been first sealed in the British Isles, and especially in Ireland. By 700 A.D. the cat was already appearing in the illuminations of the Lindisfarne Gospels, and there are numerous cat illustrations in the *Book of Kells*, produced *c.* 800 A.D. by artists working in an Irish monastery.

The Ashmolean and Harleian bestiaries of the twelfth and thirteenth centuries, although sparing with verbal descriptions, contain numerous pictures of cats, as do English Gothic psalters such as the *Luttrell Psalter* (*c.* 1330) and *Queen*

Mary's Psalter (early fourteenth century). During the same period, the French illustrator Jean Pucelle depicted a tomcat and an old man warming themselves at a fireplace, while servants stoke the fire with wood (*Psautier et Livre de Prières de Bonne de Luxembourg*, *c.* 1345), and a cat playing with a ball of yarn while a woman spins (*Livre d'Heures de Jeanne d'Evreux*, *c.* 1325).

Even the monastic rules prohibiting luxury refer to cats. The only furs permitted, for example, were the skins of sheep, rabbits, and cats. The cats in question would almost certainly have been wildcats, although we know that as early as the sixteenth century furriers were making great claims for the pelts of "Chartreux cats." There are several written references to domestic cats in monasteries.

Oddly enough, it was in the same period as the Papal bull *Vox in Rama* (1233), which launched so many cat massacres, that the animal's image was proliferating in Catholic sanctuaries thanks to the carvers of misericords in choir stalls.

More than 270 representations of animals have been catalogued in Great Britain, France, Switzerland, Belgium, Germany, and Spain. While dogs head the list, with 26 carvings, the cat has a good second place, with 15, dating from the thirteenth to the sixteenth century: an astonishing number, given the period and the almost total silence surrounding the cat in the texts of Gothic bestiaries.

The cat also infiltrated the Church via literature, with numerous scenes from the tale of *Reynard the Fox* illustrated on carved panels. Notable examples include three from Bristol Cathedral: Tybert the cat preaching (at St. Claude, in the Jura), and holding

out a missal to Bernard, and the donkey archpriest (in Strasbourg Cathedral).

Should we look on the presence of these cats, and of other subjects deemed to be improper — especially scatological ones — as deliberate provocation on the part of the artists? This seems unlikely, given that the clerics who paid for the work had to agree to the subjects, often suggesting the themes themselves.

Eglise St. Pierre (c. 1150). Marestay (Charente-Maritime), France.

FAITH HEALER OR PHYSICIAN

The priests of Bastet were well versed in the two arts that are so often inextricably linked—magic and medicine. They had a range of charms, amulets, and incantations at their disposal for the treatment of mothers and their newborn babies, and used to inject children with a few drops of cat's blood to immunize them against epidemics. Linked to Bastet in Egypt, then to Artemis in Greece and Diana in the Roman world, the cat remained the chosen companion of priestesses, soothsayers, and other prophetesses who, in the Middle Ages, were all classed as witches. A witch would be compelled, often under torture, to reveal the identity of her "familiar," who more often than not was a cat.

Why this relentless hostility to witches — and their cats? The main reason was the Church's determination to annihilate everything connected with the pagan fertility rites known as sabbats. In rural areas, women in particular would go to the wise woman rather than the priest, for she knew the art of healing with medicinal herbs, and how to deal with intimate problems of pregnancy (or, perhaps, its termination) and didn't bring morality into it. The medical profession, in its anxiety to regain its clientele, sided with the clergy. The cat had the great misfortune to be the closest companion of these old women, who, although venerated in ancient times, could not be tolerated in the Christian West because they represented a return to the bad old ways, or at least were a reminder of pagan days. Western medicine has long considered the cat a danger to health.

In the sixteenth century, Ambroise Paré, the French surgeon, described the cat as "a venomous animal which infects through its hair, its breath and its brains."

The 1763 edition of the *Encyclopédie* of Diderot and d'Alembert adopts a prudent position, to say the least:

Most medical writers report diverse qualities which many doctors have accorded to the various parts of the domestic cat as well as to his wild cousin...

The real healing power of the cat stems quite simply from its presence, as doctors and scientists are only now rediscovering. The cat works wonders in pediatric, psychiatric, and geriatric cases alike. The simple action of stroking a cat is wonderfully effective in reducing tension. The cat teaches children to be sociable, aids depressives, fills the void in the lives of the lonely, and restores old people's interest in life. This is the true therapeutic role of the cat — a gentle healing based on stroking and purring. Is the cat a magician?

CHILDREN'S STORIES

Before the eighteenth century, the cat enjoyed a clandestine life in literature. It is no accident that, at a time when religion and superstition had blackened its reputation, the animal tiptoed into favor through the side door of fairy tales. The theme taken up by Charles Perrault in *Le Chat Botté* (Puss in Boots), already well known, was echoed in the English tale of Dick Whittington. In the story, a young country boy comes to the big city to seek his fortune. He gets a job on a ship, taking his cat to sea with him. Reaching a distant country where the cat was unknown but rats, unfortunately, all too familiar, the boy makes a fortune by hiring out his companion. The grateful king showers him with gold, and he returns in triumph to London. This is a particularly positive image of the cat as a useful, affectionate, luck-bringing animal.

Charles Perrault's version is a story of utter amorality, in which a cat lies, steals, schemes, and kills for the sake of a young millhand. It is an illustration of alchemy in action. In this tale, the youngest of the miller's three sons inherits a talking cat who demands boots, so that he can pass himself off as the servant of the Marquis of Carabas. The cat lures a rabbit (the novice) into a bag, leads the king into temptation by offering him partridges (birds regarded

Palma de Falco: Two cats.

as diabolic in medieval times), dunks his protégé in the river (the purifying bath), and steals the royal clothes for him, which reveal the young man's mercurial nature to the king's daughter (the virgin). The principles of the sun and the moon can only be united by destroying the ogre, who is the incarnation of the dark forces that, without a controlling intelligence, are blindly destructive. The cat shows this when he challenges the ogre to demonstrate his magical powers by turning himself into a lion and then into a mouse — which the ogre obligingly does, with obvious results. Thus, the story ends with a celebration of the alchemical marriage, in which the cult of the moon is seen to regain its former place alongside the religion of the sun.

Through stories such as these, the cat regained the status it had once enjoyed before the upheavals of the Middle Ages. In 1945 Jean Cocteau brought *Beauty and the Beast* to the screen. Cocteau deliberately set out to give the beast a feline look. What better animal than a cat to show the conflict between a ferocious nature and an irresistible impulse to tenderness? Three centuries after Perrault, Cocteau's film proves that the magic words "Once upon a time" have lost none of their hold on our imagination.

CATS AND THE WEATHER

People have always used animal behavior to help them to predict the weather. In the case of cats, the range of indicators is limited, although the idea, for example, that a cat with its paw behind its ear is a portent of rain to come is remarkably well established in Britain, France, Italy, German-speaking Switzerland, and elsewhere.

A whole body of weather lore has grown up around the various postures of cats, often owing as much to the imagination as to the observation of behavior. A cat that purrs and rubs its nose, for example, is supposed to be a sign of good weather. When it runs around and scratches the ground, storms are said to be brewing. A nervous cat presages wind, while a yawning cat is another sign of rain. If your cat goes right up to the fireplace, bad weather is on the way, and if it turns around to toast its backside, you can expect snow.

The meteorological sensitivity of cats has been enshrined in many popular sayings. For example:

> *"When a cat washes its face*
> *The weather's about to break."*

Or:

> *"If a cat puts its paw against its ear*
> *There's no hope of fine weather."*

There is no doubt that cats do sense the approach of storms, earthquakes, cyclones, and volcanic eruptions, but there is nothing supernatural about it. Increased charges of static electricity and sudden variations of barometric pressure must have a lot to do with it. What is surprising is that no one seems to have noticed that, regardless of the weather, a cat will always put its paw behind its ear when washing.

Moritz von Schwind (1804–1871): Die Katzensymphonie (1868)

AN EAR FOR MUSIC

How could an animal that has sixty different sounds at its disposal with which to express itself be indifferent to music? The cat has been associated with music for many centuries, thanks to the subtlety of its ear, initially in ancient Egypt, in the guise of Bastet, the goddess with the sistrum. The sistrum is a rudimentary instrument, consisting of a handle, supported by the double head of the divine sisters, a circular frame across which are fixed four metallic rods carrying rings that are free to slide when the instrument is shaken. "Surmounting the frame of the sistrum," Plutarch notes, "is a carving of a cat with human features."

By placing the cat on one of the oldest of all musical instruments, the Egyptian priests were honoring the cat as the symbol of the sacred music whose rhythmic vibrations roused and alerted sleepers, while warding off evil spirits. The music inspired dancing, of which Bastet was again, appropriately, the goddess.

The association of cats with music has not been confined to Egypt. The Javanese *saron* takes the form of a seated cat, while the Japanese went even further, literally making the cat into a musical instrument — the soundbox of the *samisen* used to have cat skin stretched across it, and cats' intestines were used to make the strings, just as catgut was later used in the West for the strings of violins.

With its sensitivity to "the well-tuned voice that tells the truth," the cat has often been an accomplice to music

Sistre

making. But this should not surprise us, for we know that cats can differentiate between semitones in the lower register and are even more sensitive to the higher frequencies.

Can a cat compose music? Domenico Scarlatti (1685–1757) certainly thought so, claiming to be indebted to his cat Pulcinella for the theme of his Fugue in G minor (L499) — one of his 555 sonatas for harpsichord — which he dedicated to the Infanta Maria Barbara of Spain, and left to posterity as the Cat Fugue.

Since then the cat has often been a source of inspiration for composers. Examples include Chopin's Cat Waltz, which is supposed to represent a cat playing with a ball of wool, and *Mi-a-ou,* from Gabriel Fauré's *Dolly* (1893).

Let us examine the various instruments used to suggest cats. The harpsichord, as we have seen, was chosen by Scarlatti, the piano by Chopin, and, utilizing four hands, by Fauré, as well as by Erik Satie (*Chanson du Chat*), Darius Milhaud (*Le Chat,* five pieces for piano),

Charles-Antoine Coypel (1694–1752): engraving for "The Cats," an opera by Antoinette Deshoulières.

Henri Sauguet (for a setting of poems by Baudelaire), and Gabriel Pierné (*Trois Petits Chats Blancs*). The clarinet was used by Stravinsky in his *Berceuses du Chat*. The same instrument, in a lower register, represented the cat in Prokofiev's *Peter and the Wolf* (1936). For the feline duet in Colette's *L'Enfant et les Sortilèges* (1925), Maurice Ravel chose to support the two voices (baritone and mezzo-soprano) with *glissandi* in the string section.

The art of the musical meow, which Ravel mastered so gloriously, already had two famous precedents. The first was Mozart's duet for soprano and baritone, *Nun, liebes Weibchen* (1790), and, of course, the *Cats' Duet,* that much loved party piece of many singers, which has traditionally been attributed to Rossini, but whose origins are, in fact, obscure.

PLAYING THE CAT

"Cat and Mouse," "Cat on a Pole," "Cat's Cradle," "Puss in the Corner," "Tip-cat," "Cat-in-the-hole," "Chat-mimi-monté," "Gare au matou," "Gatta cieca"... Throughout history, children all over the world have played cat games. The ancient Egyptians had cat and mouse toys with moveable joints, and cats feature in numerous board games, card games, nursery rhymes, rounds, and riddles.

In "Cat and Rat," two children would face each other, blindfolded, both of them bound by a cord that was fixed to a point in the ground between them. The cat was armed with a stick. The rat, who was not allowed to defend himself, had to announce his presence "musically" when the cat cried out "Rat!"

Another game was "Cat and Mouse," a version of "Kiss in the Ring": the mouse was in the center of a circle; the cat, outside, tried to break through the barrier in order to steal a kiss from the mouse. This sometimes led to erotic tumbles, but once the mouse had been "eaten," a new couple would start the game again.

As if violence and sex were not enough, we can also detect an echo of sacrificial rites in "Cat!" and "Cat on a Pole," versions of the familiar game of "tag." A child chosen by lot has to pursue the other children, who climb walls, etc, to avoid being caught. The one who is seized takes the cat's place. Roger Caillois comments:

In this game, under the guise of childish innocence we can see the alarming election of a propitiatory victim or scapegoat: chosen by chance or by the meaningless, empty words of a counting rhyme, he is supposed to get rid of his taint by transmitting it, through touch, to the person he catches in the chase.

MANEKI NEKO...GOOD LUCK!

It seems almost certain that the cat was introduced into Japan as early as the sixth century A.D., probably from China or Korea. If it was originally an alien import, it is one of the few that the Japanese have taken to their hearts, boasting that in their bobtail cat, a tortoiseshell known as *mike neko*, they have the only breed on earth with a tail shaped like a chrysanthemum. As this strange creature is also credited with the power of warding off evil spirits, one can understand the pride they take in it.

In the official Japanese version, the cat came to Japan on the tenth day of the fifth month of the year 999. On that day, a Chinese mandarin presented the young emperor Idi-Jo (or Ichi-Jo) with a white female cat. When it gave birth to five kittens in the imperial palace of Kyoto, this evidence of fertility was taken to be an augury of a happy future for the cat. A thousand years later, the white cat reigns over industrial Japan, in the form of the *maneki neko*, a statuette of a tomcat, seated, with one paw raised. Examples are everywhere, from the offices of the biggest companies and banks to the most humble shop or stall, and although the figurine looks like a child's toy, no one would dream of smiling in its presence.

Why all this respect? It is only a short step from fertility to prosperity, says the *maneki neko*, or "the cat that invites" — and that is the meaning of the famous gesture, repeated by the charming cat in his formal pose. There is also a subtle distinction in its message: if the cat is raising its right paw, it is promising *fuku*, which means good luck and happiness; while the left paw ensures *sen ryo*, meaning lots of money. (The *ryo* was the gold currency of the Edo period from 1603 to 1867.) It is the cat with upraised left paw that is the universal choice of commercial enterprises.

CAT WATCHING

After suffering hundreds of years of hatred and massacre at the hands of Europeans, the cat has at last won back some of the homage it deserves. Aided by its attractive appearance and civilized habits, by the end of the nineteenth century it was firmly established as a favorite household pet. All that remained was to celebrate feline beauty in ceremonies to match the splendors of Pharaonic Egypt.

Cat mania originated in Great Britain in July 1871, when an aesthete named Harrison Weir had the idea of organizing a cat exhibition at Crystal Palace, London. It was a great success, with a crowd of visitors coming to admire the 160 cats on show. Many cat competitions were to follow, their popularity spreading worldwide, while clubs and associations in the hundreds sprang up to cater to the new enthusiasts. Universally praised for its beauty, the cat had become a favorite subject for several artists; the next step was to gain entry into the museums. This happened on June 12, 1982, when the first cat museum opened near Basel, Switzer-

land. The event was greeted by the press without even a trace of ridicule as if, suddenly, it seemed perfectly acceptable to honor the memory of the divine descendants of Bastet.

Since then, other museums have opened, in Amsterdam and in eastern France. Their documents, artifacts, and works of art bear witness to the importance of the cat in our daily lives and in our imagination, proof that at the dawn of the second millennium, man's relationship with the cat has changed from that of merciless torturer to willing and contented slave. A fitting regression, and one about which we will hear no complaints from the cats.

BREEDS OF CATS ILLUSTRATED

Extracted from *The Secret Life of Cats*

Text by Robert de Laroche • Photographs by Jean-Michel Labat

U.S. Edition ©1995 Barron's Educational Series, Inc. All rights reserved.

Library of Congress Card No. 94-46446